Editor:
Ina Massler Levin, M.A.

Senior Editor:
Sharon Coan, M.S. Ed.

Art Direction:
Elayne Roberts
Darlene Spivak

Illustrator:
Sue Fullam

Product Manager:
Phil Garcia

Imaging:
Alfred Lau
Graphics Plus

Cover Photo:
Image provided by
PhotoDisc ©1994

Publishers:
Rachelle Cracchiolo, M.S. Ed.
Mary Dupuy Smith, M.S. Ed.

SOCIAL STUDIES ASSESSMENT

GRADES 3–4

Written by
Concetta Doti Ryan, M.A.

Teacher Created Materials, Inc.
P.O. Box 1040
Huntington Beach, CA 92647
©1994 Teacher Created Materials, Inc.
Made in U.S. A.
ISBN 1-55734-776-X

Table of Contents

Introduction

Recently, there have been many changes in the way we teach social studies. The focus is no longer on reading the textbook from front cover to back and taking multiple choice tests. Instead we are making dramatic efforts to get students more interested and involved in the study of social studies. How are we doing this? We are supplementing the textbook with historical fiction, research projects, and cooperative investigations to name a few examples.

As our focus changes from memorizing facts to building a deeper understanding of historical events, we need to reevaluate our tools of assessment. Do standardized tests really measure what teachers, parents, and students need to know? Essentially what these tests really measure is the students' response to isolated, disconnected questions. To get a more complete picture of the students' progress, a more authentic form of assessment is needed; one that is in line with the new methods we are using to teach social studies. Fortunately, there are now several types of assessment that measure a student's social studies concept development in a sophisticated, detailed, and authentic manner.

Portfolios were among the first types of authentic assessment to gain ground. We teachers liked them so much because we felt as if we could really have some ownership of them. In other words, there were no specific rules for portfolios. We designed the portfolio to match the needs of our students, our classroom, and our assessment procedures.

Recently, other types of authentic assessment have begun gaining popularity, particularly performance assessment. Performance assessment evaluates students in a variety of contexts by allowing them to apply knowledge and skills, and demonstrate the understanding of concepts they have acquired.

While many teachers acknowledge that authentic assessment is no easy task, it is certainly worth the effort. Fortunately, resource guides such as this are making it easier for teachers to use more authentic types of assessment in their classrooms.

Introduction (cont.)

This resource guide will help you implement authentic assessment in your classroom immediately. It provides both theoretical information and ideas for practical application. The types of authentic assessment covered include:

★ **Portfolios**

★ **Logs and Journals**

★ **Performance Assessment and Rubrics**

★ **Cooperative Investigations**

★ **Research Projects**

★ **Student Self-Evaluation**

★ **Parent Evaluation**

Along with these seven detailed sections, you will find information on **Social Studies Program Evaluation** and **Social Studies Skills and Concepts Development Evaluation**. Each section begins with "Getting Started." Here you will find the following topics:

Rationale: Theoretical information on that type of authentic assessment.

How to: Ideas for how to implement that type of authentic assessment.

Using the Forms in This Section: Instructions for using every assessment form included in that section.

For each type of authentic assessment in this resource guide, you will find several blackline forms for immediate use in your classroom. Also included are a generic record sheet, a student award form, and a social studies assessment bibliography.

With this extensive resource guide you should feel confident about implementing an authentic assessment program in your classroom. It will be worth it to you, the parents, and most of all, the students!

Getting Started

Rationale

As you transition from a more traditional type of assessment to authentic assessment in social studies, it may be necessary to carefully examine the types of supplemental materials you use, activities you assign, units of study, your own methods of teaching, and your personal beliefs about assessment.

Have you ever become frustrated by your students' lack of interest in social studies? Well, you are not alone! In 1988 a study reported that students at all grade levels identified social studies as their most boring class and cited texts as one of the major reasons for this. In order to "turn kids on" to social studies, it is necessary to go beyond mere memorization of facts from the textbook. This can be done by supplementing the text with different types of literature and primary sources.

The types of literature you may wish to include in your program are biographies, historical fiction, myths, and legends. Primary sources include items such as letters, speeches, and diaries. We also need to provide more authentic projects that allow students to take an active role in their studies. Students can be encouraged to do research projects requiring them to go into the community and interview residents about certain issues or topics. Their findings can be written up in a report or used as part of a larger project involving the research from several students. These types of supplements and activities make social studies come alive for students and teachers.

How to Evaluate Your Social Studies Program

When evaluating your social studies program, you should consider the types of literature and primary sources you use to supplement the text, the activities and projects you assign, and the visual supplements you use to help students understand concepts such as maps, globes, and timelines.

You may also choose to do a self-evaluation. If we want students to take part in their evaluation, why not become involved in our own? Consider what you are teaching, why you are teaching it, and how you are teaching it. Then, consider how you assess what you teach. Does your assessment tool measure what you need it to measure?

Also consider evaluating the thematic units you use. Do they support the curriculum in the textbook? Was the unit successful with the students? By evaluating these units you will be better prepared to plan your curriculum for the next school year.

Getting Started (cont.) _____

Using the Forms in This Section

Social Studies Activity Assessment, Page 7

Evaluate the supplements you use and the activities you assign by answering "yes" or "no" to the questions included on this activity assessment page.

Teacher Self-Evaluation, Page 8

It is not always easy to look at our own teaching with a critical eye. However, by doing so we gain insight into the program we provide for our students. This self-evaluation will ask you to consider the choices you give students, your expectations for students, and your communication skills to name just a few examples.

Personal Beliefs About Assessment, Page 9

Before deciding which types of authentic assessment you want to implement in your classroom, it is important to think about your beliefs and goals for assessment. Use this form to note those personal beliefs and goals. Several example statements are given below:

> Evaluation needs to be on-going, informal and formal, clearly defined, noncompetitive.

> Evaluation procedures should be based on daily observations, include process and product, consider parent and student input.

Thematic Unit Evaluation, Page 10

This form is designed to assist you in keeping track of your thematic units, their degree of success, and changes you may wish to make for the following year.

6

Social Studies Activity Assessment

Check yes or no for each question.

	Yes	No
Use of Literature		
Biographies	_____	_____
Myths	_____	_____
Historical Fiction	_____	_____
Legends	_____	_____
Poems	_____	_____
Use of Original Documents/ Primary Sources		
Newspaper Accounts	_____	_____
Court Decisions	_____	_____
Letters	_____	_____
Speeches	_____	_____
Diaries	_____	_____
Other Official Documents	_____	_____
Interactive Projects/Activities		
Oral History Projects	_____	_____
Debates	_____	_____
Simulations	_____	_____
Role Playing	_____	_____
Cooperative Learning Tasks	_____	_____
Research Projects	_____	_____
Interviews	_____	_____
Journal Writing	_____	_____
Use of Visual Supplements		
Maps	_____	_____
Globe	_____	_____
Timelines	_____	_____
Charts	_____	_____
Diagrams	_____	_____

Teacher Self-Evaluation

Answer yes or no to each question.

_____ Does social studies have a significant role in my curriculum?

_____ Do I use historical fiction to supplement the text?

_____ Do I use primary sources to supplement the text?

_____ Do I provide assignments that require critical thinking skills?

_____ Do I ask open-ended questions?

_____ Do I listen carefully to students' responses?

_____ Do I respect students' responses?

_____ Do I have high expectations for all students?

_____ Do I thoroughly explain evaluation criteria?

_____ Do students in the class feel successful?

_____ Do I comment on students' strengths?

_____ Do I offer suggestions for improvement?

_____ Do I provide time for student interaction and sharing?

_____ Do I encourage students to take responsibility for their learning?

_____ Do I allow students to self-evaluate?

_____ Do I encourage parents to participate in the evaluation of their child?

_____ Do I communicate effectively with students?

_____ Do I communicate effectively with parents?

My strengths are: _____

_____

_____

I would like to improve: _____

_____

_____

Personal Beliefs About Assessment

Use this form to note your personal beliefs and goals for social studies assessment in your classroom. For sample statements, see page 6.

Beliefs:	**Goals:**
Evaluation needs to be...	Evaluation procedures should...

Thematic Unit Evaluation

Unit Title	Unit Description	Date	Degree of Success	Changes for Next Year

Getting Started

Rationale

It is important that we look at a student's understanding of social studies skills and concepts over time. By making sure that we are covering the necessary skills, we can better assure that students are understanding larger social studies concepts. Therefore, we should keep close record of required grade level skills, the unit in which these skills are covered, and how we assess these skills. We should then take careful note of student's concept development, at least once each quarter, so that progress and growth can be tracked, and more importantly, encouraged. This need not be a time consuming process. In fact, completing a simple checklist can be as easy as 1-2-3.

How to Evaluate Social Studies Skills and Concepts

Your first step is to identify the skills you are required to teach at your grade level. A comprehensive checklist of skills for both grades three and four is provided in this resource guide. Grade three can be found on pages 13 through 18. Grade four can be found on pages 19 through 24. This checklist allows you to keep track of the unit in which each skill is taught, the dates on which the unit is expected to be taught, and the form of assessment for the skill.

After charting the skills you are teaching, you can begin observing students for evidence of an understanding of larger social studies concepts. Students should be "watched" or observed in a variety of settings and activities. Observe them during instructional time, free time, working by themselves, with partners, or in small groups, and with best friends. Observe students anywhere and anytime you can! As you observe students, mark on the comprehensive checklist on pages 25 through 27 to indicate what you saw at that time.

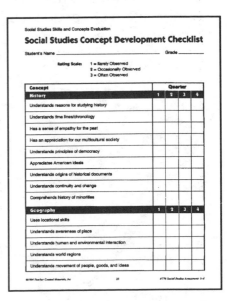

Getting Started (cont.) _____

Using the Forms in This Section

Social Studies Skills Checklist: Grade 3, Page 13

This comprehensive checklist identifies grade three social studies skills for 14 different strands, including history, geography, economics, culture, ethics and belief systems, social and political systems, national identity, constitutional heritage, citizenship, study skills, visual learning, map and globe skills, critical thinking, and social participation. For each skill in each strand you are asked to identify the unit in which the skill is covered, the date the unit will be taught, and how the skill will be assessed.

Social Studies Skills Checklist: Grade 4, Page 19

This comprehensive checklist identifies grade four social studies skills for 14 different strands, including history, geography, economics, culture, ethics and belief systems, social and political systems, national identity, constitutional heritage, citizenship, study skills, visual learning, map and globe skills, critical thinking, and social participation. For each skill in each strand, you are asked to identify in which unit the skill is covered, the date the unit will be taught, and how the skill will be assessed.

Social Studies Concept Development Checklist, Page 25

This comprehensive checklist can be invaluable to you as a "kidwatcher." It is convenient and quick to use and provides space for reporting on students each quarter. The following categories are included on the checklist: history, geography, citizenship, critical thinking, participation skills, and study skills. Several blank lines are provided for additional skills you would like to add.

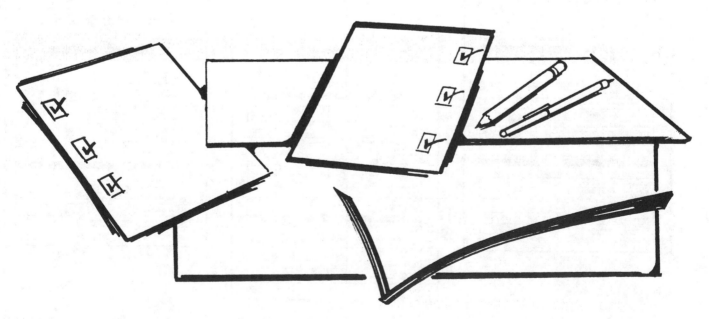

Social Studies Skills and Concepts Evaluation

Social Studies Skills Checklist: Grade 3

Teacher's Name _____

School Year _____

Skill	Date	Unit	Form of Assessment
History			
Discusses traditions and their origins			
Reads journals of pioneers			
Is familiar with real people of the past			
Reads and uses time lines			
Understands migration and settlement			
Recognizes conservation issues			
Sees the interrelatedness of geography			
Appreciates diversity of people			
Is knowledgeable about bust of a boom town			
Geography			
Understands relative location			
Identifies place characteristics			
Is aware of environmental changes in community interactions			
Participates in community interactions			
Is aware of historical movement of people			
Identifies regional characteristics			

Social Studies Skills Checklist: Grade 3 (cont.)

Skill	Date	Unit	Form of Assessment
Economics			
Discusses how needs are met over time			
Understands Native American exchange systems			
Sees the connection between production and distribution			
Recognizes interdependence of communities			
Sees the connection between production and transportation			
Culture			
Is familiar with how cultural understanding is transmitted			
Appreciates cultural complexity of Native Americans			
Listens and responds to literature of other times and places			
Listens and responds to myths of Native Americans			
Listens and responds to legends of Native Americans			
Listens and responds to myths of cowboys and settlers			
Listens and responds to legends of cowboys and settlers			

Social Studies Skills Checklist: Grade 3 (cont.)

Skill	Date	Unit	Form of Assessment
Ethics and Belief Systems			
Is aware of ethics and beliefs in Native American societies			
Is aware of influence of religion among Native Americans			
Recognizes influence of religion among Pilgrims			
Knows basic belief system of Native Americans			
Discusses resolution of ethical issues in literature			
Social and Political Systems			
Understands responsibility of individuals to group			
Recognizes there are rules of law in other societies			
Discusses opposing ideals of Native Americans and settlers			
Is aware of social structure in other times			
Identifies differing political systems			
Is aware of international trade			

Social Studies Skills Checklist: Grade 3 (cont.)

Skill	Date	Unit	Form of Assessment
National Identity			
Recognizes examples of pluralism			
Understands democracy through historical examples			
Understands democracy through contemporary examples			
Recognizes national symbols			
Knows the Pledge of Allegiance			
Knows patriotic songs			
Appreciates conservation of resources			
Constitutional Heritage			
Recognizes balance of power in other societies			
Citizenship			
Appreciates conservation of natural resources			
Respects the need for rules			
Is aware of President's Day			
Knows examples of human rights in the past			
Takes part in settlement of disputes			
Knows strategies for pluralism			

Social Studies Skills Checklist: Grade 3 (cont.)

Skill	Date	Unit	Form of Assessment
Study Skills			
Uses a library			
Uses reference materials			
Interviews for information			
Summarizes a paragraph			
Identifies main idea			
Tells events in sequence			
Writes simple paragraphs			
Visual Learning			
Observes community features			
Reads and makes time lines			
Reads charts and tables			
Reads line and circle graphs			
Reads diagrams			
Gathers information from photos			
Recognizes national symbols, flag			
Map And Globe Skills			
Reads physical map			
Uses map key, compass rose			
Uses latitude and longitude			
Follows routes on map			
Uses map scale for time and distance			

Social Studies Skills Checklist: Grade 3 (cont.)

Skill	Date	Unit	Form of Assessment
Critical Thinking			
Identifies problem			
Identifies central issue			
Provides evidence to support main idea			
Identifies cause and effect			
Social Participation			
Recognizes other's point of view			
Expresses one's own ideas			
Identifies goal of group work			
Accepts group decisions			
Other			

Social Studies Skills and Concepts Evaluation

Social Studies Skills Checklist: Grade 4

Teacher's Name _____

School Year _____

Skill	Date	Unit	Form of Assessment
History			
Knows state and region place names			
Is aware of family history			
Uses primary sources			
Uses artifacts			
Knows past settlers of the state			
Understands settlement and expansion			
Reads and uses time lines			
Appreciates cultural diversity			
Recognizes changes in region			
Sees the interrelatedness of geography, economics, religion, and culture			
Comprehends the role of minorities in early U.S. society			
Geography			
Recognizes factors that influence location			
Knows the difference between rural vs. urban areas			
Is aware of environmental changes in the community			
Knows reasons for migration			
Identifies nature and characteristics of regions			

Social Studies Skills Checklist: Grade 4 (cont.)

Skill	Date	Unit	Form of Assessment
Economics			
Knows basic history of businesses			
Understands the use of barter			
Understands money flow			
Understands economic cycles			
Recognizes interdependence of regions			
Comprehends the effect of natural disasters			
Appreciates World War II technology			
Culture			
Is familiar with how cultural understanding is transmitted			
Appreciates cultural complexity of state and region			
Listens and responds to literature and art throughout area's history			
Listens and responds to myths of Native Americans			
Listens and responds to legends of Native Americans			
Listens and responds to myths of cowboys and settlers			
Listens and responds to legends of cowboys and settlers			

Social Studies Skills Checklist: Grade 4 (cont.)

Skill	Date	Unit	Form of Assessment
Ethic and Belief Systems			
Is aware of ethic and belief systems in history of state, region, and country			
Knows role of missionaries			
Respects beliefs of immigrants			
Discusses conflict between belief systems			
Knows belief systems of Native Americans			
Discusses resolution of ethical issues in literature			
Social and Political Systems			
Is familiar with political sub-units			
Respects law enforcement			
Recognizes conflicting goals in state and regional history			
Identifies differences in social structures over time			
Is aware of variety of political systems			
Recognizes interdependence of trade and foreign affairs			

Social Studies Skills Checklist: Grade 4 (cont.)

Skill	Date	Unit	Form of Assessment
National Identity			
Recognizes examples of pluralism			
Comprehends historic examples of democracy			
Comprehends contemporary examples of democracy			
Recognizes state symbols			
Predicts state or region's future			
Constitutional Heritage			
Understands balance of power in state			
Is familiar with state constitution			
Is aware of changes in state laws over time			
Citizenship			
Respects the need for rules			
Is familiar with rule violations in past			
Understands the process of selecting state leaders			
Is aware of human rights in state history			
Discusses conflict resolution in state history			
Understands pluralism in state history			

22

Social Studies Skills Checklist: Grade 4 (cont.)

Skill	Date	Unit	Form of Assessment
Study Skills			
Uses library catalog			
Interviews for information			
Combines information			
Gives directions			
Possesses oral discussion skills			
Plans reports			
Writes reports			
Visual Learning			
Observes regional features			
Reads time zone maps			
Reads time lines			
Reads charts and tables			
Reads bar, line, and circle graphs			
Reads diagrams			
Interprets material			
Recognizes state symbols			
Map and Globe Skills			
Makes map symbols			
Understands hemispheres			
Understands global reference points			
Knows directional terms			
Makes a map			

Social Studies Skills Checklist: Grade 4 (cont.)

Skill	Date	Unit	Form of Assessment
Critical Thinking			
Identifies the problems			
Identifies the central issues			
Distinguishes between fact and opinions			
Evaluates information			
Identifies cause and effect			
Draws conclusions			
Social Participation			
Listens to others			
Expresses one's own ideas			
Participates in discussions			
Other			

24

Social Studies Concept Development Checklist

Student's Name _____ Grade _____

Rating Scale: 1 = Rarely Observed
                      2 = Occasionally Observed
                      3 = Often Observed

Concept	Quarter			
History	**1**	**2**	**3**	**4**
Understands reasons for studying history				
Understands time lines/chronology				
Has a sense of empathy for the past				
Has an appreciation for our multicultural society				
Understands principles of democracy				
Appreciates American ideals				
Understands origins of historical documents				
Understands continuity and change				
Comprehends history of minorities				
Geography	**1**	**2**	**3**	**4**
Uses locational skills				
Understands awareness of place				
Understands human and environmental interaction				
Understands world regions				
Understands movement of people, goods, and ideas				

Social Studies Concept Development (cont.)

Concept	Quarter			
Citizenship	**1**	**2**	**3**	**4**
Understands duties of our leaders				
Understands selection of our leaders				
Respects human rights of individuals and minorities				
Understands responsibility of being a citizen in a democratic society				
Shows commitment to democratic values				
Understands conflict resolution				
Understands factors leading to the fall of some democracies				
Critical Thinking Skills	**1**	**2**	**3**	**4**
Defines central issues/problems				
Clarifies central issues/problems				
Evaluates information related to a problem				
Solves problems				
Draws conclusions related to an issue				
Participation Skills	**1**	**2**	**3**	**4**
Expresses personal convictions				
Listens to differing points of view				
Develops interpersonal skills				
Works successfully in groups				
Speaks confidently				

Social Studies Concept Development (cont.)

Concept	Quarter			
Study Skills	**1**	**2**	**3**	**4**
Locates information				
Selects appropriate information				
Acquires information by:				
listening				
observing				
interviewing				
reading literature				
consulting primary sources				
Reads and interprets:				
maps				
globes				
diagrams				
graphs				
charts				
time lines				
Other	**1**	**2**	**3**	**4**

Getting Started

Rationale

As our philosophy and teaching methods for social studies change, we become aware of the need for a more authentic means of assessment. One such approach to process evaluation is the portfolio. Portfolios represent a philosophy that demands we view assessment as an integral part of instruction. It is an expanded definition of assessment in which a variety of indicators of learning are gathered across many situations. It is a philosophy that honors both the process and the products of learning, as well as the active participation of the teacher and the students.

What will ultimately be included in the portfolio is up to you and your students. Suggestions include student work samples, self-evaluations, interest inventories, surveys, and anecdotal records.

How to Use Portfolios

The first step in beginning to use portfolios in your classroom is determining their purpose. The purpose will depend on the assessment needs in your classroom. Use the questions below to help you establish the purpose for the use of portfolios in your own classroom.

- Will the portfolio be a collection of work or a sample of the student's best work?
- Will the portfolio contain finished products only?
- Will the portfolio be passed on to the next teacher?
- Who will select what is included in the portfolio?
- Who will have access to the portfolio?
- How will students be involved with the portfolio?

The next step is to consider where the portfolios will be housed. Depending on your purpose, you may or may not want students to have access to the portfolio. If the portfolio is exclusively for your use, store it in a file cabinet that students do not have access to. On the other hand, if you want students to contribute to their portfolios, keep them in a highly visible place in the classroom. In either case, each student should have a clearly marked file folder to hold the contents of the portfolio. To help establish interest and ownership of the portfolio, allow students to decorate their portfolio folder any way they wish.

28

Getting Started (cont.) _____

Now that you have determined your purpose and set up the portfolio filing system, you must decide on what will be included in the portfolio. The possibilities include student work samples, self-evaluations, interest inventories, surveys, and anecdotal records, just to name a few. In this section of the resource guide, you will find forms for students to record and evaluate their portfolio selections, an interest inventory, a social studies survey as well as a blank form to create your own, and three types of anecdotal record forms. However, all the forms found in this assessment resource guide would be appropriate for the student's portfolio.

The final step in the portfolio process would be to decide how you will analyze the contents. Having established criteria will greatly help you when report card time rolls around. You can use these criteria to review the contents of the portfolio and to make a formal grade, if your school requires that you give grades. Some schools are moving toward a narrative-type report card in which single grades give way to brief essays regarding a student's progress. With this type of grading system, portfolios become an invaluable part of student assessment.

Using the Forms in This Section

Portfolio Activity Sample Cover Sheet, Page 32

If you allow students to take part in the selection of portfolio contents, this form can be very useful. The students attach this form to the top of a work sample they have selected for inclusion in their portfolio. On it they write the title of the assignment, why it was selected for the portfolio, and what they like best about their performance on the assignment.

Portfolio Record Keeping, Page 33

This form can be used by students to keep track of the assignments they have chosen for their portfolio for each unit of study. For each of three units of study, students are asked to choose three activities for inclusion in their portfolio, as well as selecting which was their favorite activity.

Getting Started (cont.) _____

Portfolio Content Analysis, Page 34

After all portfolio items have been collected, you will want to analyze the student's progress. This narrative form allows you to make notes regarding a student's performance on classroom work, research projects, cooperative investigations, written products, and self-evaluations. This information can then be transferred to a narrative report card, comment section of a traditional report card, or used as support for report card grades during parent conferences.

Interest Inventory, Page 35

Interest inventories allow teachers to find out basic information about students' likes, dislikes, hobbies, and friends. Interest inventories can be particularly valuable at the beginning of the year when you are getting to know each of your students. The information can help you plan thematic units based on the topics your students are interested in. If you feel that your students cannot complete this inventory on their own, solicit the help of parent volunteers.

Social Studies Survey, Page 36

Surveys are also valuable at the beginning of the year. However, if you use surveys over time, say at the beginning of the year and then again several months later, you may notice changing attitudes and interests that can again help in curriculum planning. Survey students' attitudes toward the study of history. Find out what they enjoy about the subject and what frustrates them. This survey can also determine if students understand the importance of studying the past.

Student Survey, Page 37

This blank form can be used to create your own survey on a topic of your choice. There is room for you to write in four different questions for students to answer. Below is an example of survey questions:

1. Would you like to learn about Native Americans?

2. What do you already know about Native Americans?

3. What would you like to know about Native Americans?

30

Getting Started (cont.) _____

Anecdotal Record Form #1, Page 38

Anecdotal notes and observations are carefully documented records of certain events, behaviors, and skills. They provide a record you can review independently or share with parents during conference time. When these notes and observations are put together, they tell an on-going story about the student's growth and progress. This form can be used to record information on a single student about a specific event. The first three observations are objective, simply asking you to record information. The final question asks you to be interpretive and identify why the behavior is important.

Portfolios

Anecdotal Record Form #1

Student's Name: *Cheryl Preece*   Date: *5/19*

Subject: *Social Studies*

Instructional Situation	*Small group discussions.*
Instructional Task	*Read and discuss Native American story from the text.*
Behavior Observed	*Cheryl dominated the discussion and often interrupted others when speaking.*
This behavior was important because	*Cheryl's dominance doesn't allow group interaction. Place her carefully when determining groups next time.*

#776 Social Studies Assessment: 3–4   38   *©1994 Teacher Created Materials, Inc.*

Anecdotal Record Form #2, Page 39

This form can also be used to record information on a single student, but it has space to note several observations. It is important to date each observation.

Anecdotal Record Form #3, Page 40

This anecdotal record form can be used to record information about all students in your class. Again, it is important to note the date of your observations. This form is both objective and interpretive, asking for a description of the incident and also its possible implications.

Portfolio Activity Sample Cover Sheet

Name _____

Date _____

Title of assignment:

_____

Why did you choose this assignment for your portfolio?

_____

_____

_____

What do you like about your performance on this assignment?

_____

_____

_____

_____

Portfolio Record Keeping

Name _____

Unit One _____

       Activity 1 _____

       Activity 2 _____

       Activity 3 _____

My favorite activity was: _____

Unit Two _____

       Activity 1 _____

       Activity 2 _____

       Activity 3 _____

My favorite activity was: _____

Unit Three _____

       Activity 1 _____

       Activity 2 _____

       Activity 3 _____

My favorite activity was: _____

Portfolio Content Analysis

Student's Name _____ Date _____

Research Projects:

Cooperative Investigations:

Written Products:

Self-Evaluations:

Interest Inventory

Name _____

Date _____

1. What is your favorite subject in school?_____

2. What is your least favorite subject in school?_____

3. What do you like to do in your free time?_____

4. Who is your best friend?_____

5. What is your favorite sport?_____

6. What is your favorite animal? _____

7. Name something you do very well._____

8. Name something that makes you angry._____

9. What is your favorite T.V. show?_____

10. What is your favorite book?_____

11. What is your favorite movie?_____

12. If you could meet a famous person, who would it be?_____

13. Why would you like to meet that person?_____

14. What would you like to be when you grow up? _____

15. What would you like to learn in school this year? _____

Social Studies Survey

Name _____

Date _____

1. How do you feel about studying history?

   _____

   _____

2. Is it important to know about the past?

   _____

   _____

3. Is it important to know about other people and cultures?

   _____

   _____

4. What do you enjoy about the study of history?

   _____

   _____

5. What is hard about studying history?

   _____

   _____

6. What would you like to learn about in social studies this year?

   _____

   _____

Student Survey

Name _____

Date _____

1. _____

_____

_____

_____

_____

2. _____

_____

_____

_____

_____

3. _____

_____

_____

_____

_____

Anecdotal Record Form #1

Student's Name: _____ Date: _____

Subject: _____

Instructional Situation	
Instructional Task	
Behavior Observed	
This behavior was important because	

Anecdotal Record Form #2

Student's Name: _____

Date	Observation:	Watch for:

Anecdotal Record Form #3

Name	Date	Activity	Implication

Getting Started _____

Rationale

To enhance student understanding of historical events and provide motivation, students should be encouraged to read a historical novel for each unit of study. With an abundant selection of historical literature available, students can self-select the novels they will read. However, if we allow students to select their own books to read, how do we keep track of their progress? Student logs and journals can be an excellent way of charting student work, progress, and attitude for self-selected novels, and for whole class studies of particular novels.

Reading logs are designed to track progress and time spent reading. The time allotted to complete the reading is set by the teacher and may include the time spent during a particular unit of study, or simple tracking by month. A journal is one step beyond a log. In journals students are asked to respond to the books they are reading rather than just keeping a list of the titles. By reading the students' journals you can get a good idea not only of their reading comprehension, but also of their abilities to communicate in writing and to understand historical concepts. Motivation for keeping the journal comes from your written response to the student. When teachers and students write back and forth to each other, a more personal relationship can develop. With class sizes constantly increasing, the journal may be the only opportunity for the teacher and students to have a one-to-one correspondence on a regular basis. Students will appreciate this special attention.

How to Use Logs and Journals

The log is simple and merely requires that students record what they have read during a period of time. The reading log included in this guide is for a one-month period, but you can adjust that if you wish.

As stated earlier, journals have a more complex purpose. After students read a story on their own or as a class, you may ask them to respond to the story in their journals. You may wish to use the questions below. Other suggestions are provided in the "Literature Response Guide" on page 46.

☞ What was the story about?

☞ What details do you remember of the story?

☞ Where did the story take place?

☞ During what time period did the story take place?

☞ Who were the people in the story?

☞ Did you like the story?

☞ Was the story historically accurate?

Getting Started *(cont.)* _____

After the student has responded to the story in the journal, it is important that you read the response and write back. This motivates the student to continue journal writing. After the student writes several responses in the journal, you can begin the evaluation process. Read the responses and then use the "Reading Journal Evaluation" form on page 48. One final note, it may be important for you to stress the confidentiality of logs and journals to students. They will often write personal responses and should feel assured that you will be the only one to read them.

Using the Forms in This Section

Monthly Reading Log, Page 44

Use this form to help students track their independent reading of historical fiction and nonfiction during a one-month period. When students complete this form, you gain a better idea of their use of independent time in class.

Book Review, Page 45

This book review form allows the students to become book critics. They are asked why they chose the book and to briefly summarize the story. Then, they are asked to rate the book. Finally, they are asked if the book was historically accurate, which is very important in making connections between the literature and social studies concepts.

Literature Response Guide, Page 46

Students can be given this guide to assist them in writing quality literature responses for their journals. The first step asks the students to summarize with details. Then, there are seven questions that require students to react to the story.

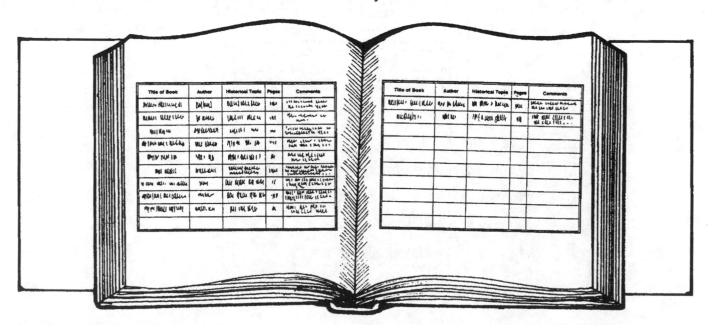

Getting Started (cont.) _____

Dialectical Journal, Page 47

This double entry journal asks students to note and respond to text in the novel that was powerful to them. It may be for historical reasons, or it may be for personal reasons that a bit of text had special meaning to the student. The importance of this journal is that the students decide what is powerful based on their own background and experiences. Again, as with other journals, your personal response to the student is both motivating and appreciated.

Reading Journal Evaluation, Page 48

If you ask students to keep a journal of their responses to books read, you will need a way to assess these responses. The "Reading Journal Evaluation" is an excellent way of reviewing what the students have written and determining their level of comprehension. The evaluation also considers their ability to communicate in writing and their understanding of historical concepts.

Facts and Feelings Chart, Page 49

This chart is particularly important in helping students make the connection between facts in the history textbook and feelings in historical novels. The fact portion of this chart is completed by students as they read their textbook. The feelings/reactions portion of the chart is completed as students read a novel about that time period. Understanding feelings and reactions to historical events helps make the events more real to students rather than just "something that happened a long time ago." It also helps students to realize consequences and repercussions of historical events that they may not understand by simply reading the textbook.

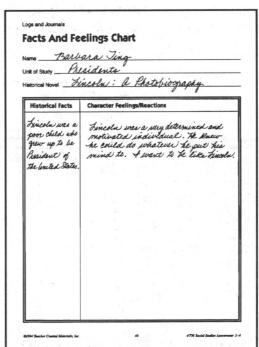

Monthly Reading Log

Use this form to record all the reading you do in one month.

Name: _____

Month: _____

Title of Book	Author	Historical Topic	Pages	Comments

What was your favorite book of the month?_____

_____

What do you plan to read next month? _____

_____

44   ©1994 Teacher Created Materials, Inc.

Book Review

Title of book _____

Author _____ Number of pages _____

Historical Topic _____

1. Why did you choose this book?

   _____

2. Summarize the story.

   _____

   _____

   _____

3. How do you rate this book?

   _____ Exciting
   _____ Interesting
   _____ O.K.
   _____ Dull

4. Was the book historically accurate? Give examples.

   _____

   _____

   _____

   _____

Reviewer's signature _____

Literature Response Guide

Name _____

Date _____

Use this guide to assist you in literature response journal writing.

Step One
Summary

Summarize the story in your own words including details of characters, main events, setting, historical time period, climax, and resolution.

Step Two
Your Reactions

1. How did the main character feel when faced with a problem?

2. Why did the character react the way he or she did?

3. What would you have done?

4. What did you like about the book?

5. What did you dislike about the book?

6. If you were the writer, what would you change?

7. Did the author make you feel that you were transported to that particular time in history?

Dialectical Journal

Name _____

Book _____

Date	Text	Response

Logs and Journals

Reading Journal Evaluation

Student's Name _____

Date of Evaluation _____ Number of Entries _____

1. Can the reader communicate in writing? _____

   Examples: _____

   _____

   _____

2. Can the reader recall details about the story? _____

   Examples: _____

   _____

   _____

3. Does the reader appear to understand story elements such as setting, character, and plot?

   Examples: _____

   _____

   _____

4. Does the reader give a supported opinion of the story? _____

   Examples: _____

   _____

   _____

5. Does the reader understand the historical concepts? _____

   Examples: _____

   _____

   _____

Other observations:

Facts And Feelings Chart

Name _____

Unit of Study _____

Historical Novel _____

Historical Facts	Character Feelings/Reactions

Getting Started

Rationale

Performance assessment is a means to evaluate students in a variety of contexts by allowing them to demonstrate their understanding of concepts and apply knowledge and skills they have acquired. Performance assessment tasks are carefully constructed in order to assess specific declarative and procedural knowledge as well as critical thinking skills. Declarative knowledge refers to facts about certain persons, places, and things, and generalizations or concepts that can be derived based on those facts. Procedural knowledge refers to skills and strategies. The tasks used to assess this knowledge are scored based on grading rubrics that are, in most cases, established by the teacher prior to introducing the task.

A rubric is a set of criteria the student sees prior to the performance task. The rubric identifies the qualities the teacher expects to see in a response at several points along a scale. By establishing the criteria prior to the activity, the student clearly knows what is expected in order to receive a specific score. Each score on the rubric is matched to an example of a response.

A rubric can be used in two ways: as an assessment tool and as a teaching tool. When a rubric is used as an assessment tool, it serves as a standard against which a sample of student work can be measured. When a rubric is used as a teaching tool, it provides an example for students to follow and can actually promote learning by offering clear performance standards for students.

How to use Performance Assessments and Rubrics

The construction of a performance task can be a time consuming process. However, with practice the tasks become easier to write. Moreover, the tasks can be used from one year to the next so you will not have to recreate a whole new set of tasks each school year.

50

Getting Started (cont.) _____

The first step in creating a performance task is to determine what content knowledge you wish to assess. Then you should determine if this content knowledge is declarative or procedural. If you are assessing declarative knowledge, your task should require students to respond in some fashion to a generalization. Students will then respond to this generalization according to the task, using their knowledge of basic facts. If you are assessing procedural knowledge, students should be required to apply a strategy such as a problem solving strategy. In their application of this strategy, they must naturally apply their knowledge of basic skills. Also consider what critical thinking skills students will have to use in order to complete the performance task.

Next you must determine the type of performance task you will use to assess the declarative or procedural knowledge. Examples of twelve types of performance assessment are explained on page 54. Once you have made all the important decisions about knowledge to assess, you can write the task. Like any other piece of writing, it may take several drafts before you are completely satisfied. You should also include in the task the way in which the students will present their findings or answer. Some presentation ideas may include a written report, a letter to an official, a debate, or a videotape.

Once you have completed writing the task, you must develop a rubric to score student responses. At this level you may wish to have three to four categories of performance standards on your rubric. There are several examples of performance tasks and rubrics in this resource guide to assist you—specifically, a decision making task, a problem solving task, and an invention task.

The task and the rubric should be established and discussed clearly with students prior to the activity. Keep in mind that the burden of establishing criteria does not always have to rest upon the teacher. Students' opinions can be solicited prior to establishing the rubric. A blank rubric form has been included in this resource guide to use when allowing students to participate in rubric development. By assisting in the creation of a rubric, students become more aware of task expectations and may therefore perform better.

Getting Started (cont.)

Using the Forms in This Section

Performance Task Types and Descriptions, Page 54

This page describes twelve types of performance assessment tasks that can be used to evaluate students in social studies. Examples of three of these are included in this section of the resource guide.

Decision Making Task, Page 55

This performance task asks students to determine the factors that may have caused lawmakers to pass the Pigtail Ordinance of the late 1800's, as well as the law's effects. This activity leads to an understanding of the larger concept of discrimination against immigrants and minorities. Background information on the Pigtail Ordinance is provided, and the task is described for students in great detail.

Decision Making Task Activity Sheet, Page 56

This activity sheet is used by students to record their responses to the task described on page 55. Students are asked what factors may have caused lawmakers to pass the Pigtail Ordinance, how it discriminates against Chinese, and the effects it may have had on Chinese immigration.

Decision Making Task Rubric, Page 57

As described earlier, for every performance task a rubric is needed in order to score the students' product. This rubric is specifically written for the decision making task on page 55.

Problem Solving Task, Page 58

The second example of performance assessment asks students to consider basic solutions to pollution problems. Their solutions have to be practical enough for the average citizen to do. General information on smoke and trash pollution is provided, and then the task is described for students in great detail.

Problem Solving Activity Task Sheet, Page 59

This page will assist students in gathering their ideas prior to creating a poster about solutions to pollution as described in the problem solving task on page 58.

Getting Started (cont.) _____

Problem Solving Task Rubric, Page 60

This rubric is specifically designed for the problem solving task on page 58.

Invention Task, Page 61

This performance task asks students to create a symbol for a national holiday of their choice. Background information on several national symbols is provided as well as a detailed explanation of the task.

Invention Task Activity Sheet, Page 62

This activity sheet allows students to record the origins of the holiday they chose and to sketch their symbol idea.

Invention Task Rubric, Page 63

This rubric was specifically designed for the invention task on page 61.

Create a Task, Page 64

Using the theoretical information provided in the "Getting Started" portion of this section and the examples of performance assessment provided, you can create your own performance assessment task for a specific unit your students are studying. This blank is just like the examples provided for ease and convenience.

Create a Rubric, Page 65

If you create your own performance assessment task, you will also need to create your own rubric. This page is just like the rubric pages used in the examples.

Performance Task Recording Sheet, Page 66

This sheet can be used to record student grades on each of the 12 types of performance assessment tasks.

Individual Student Performance Task Recording Sheet, Page 67

This narrative record sheet can be used to record a student's strengths and weaknesses on a performance task. There is space for notes about what you would like to work on to improve that student's performance.

Performance Task Types and Descriptions

Comparison Task: The student is required to compare two or more people, places, or things.

Classification Task: The student is asked to classify, or put into categories, certain people, places, or things.

Position Support Task: The student is asked to take a position on a subject or issue and defend it.

Application Task: The student is asked to apply his or her knowledge in a new situation.

Analyzing Perspectives Task: The student is asked to analyze two to three different perspectives and then choose one he or she supports.

Decision Making Task: The student must identify the factors that caused a certain decision.

Historical Perspective Task: The student must consider differing theories to answer basic historical questions.

Predictive Task: The student must make predictions about what could happen or will happen in the future.

Problem Solving Task: The student must create a solution to a specific problem.

Experimental Task: The student sets up an experiment to test a hypothesis.

Invention Task: The student must create something new and unique.

Error Identification Task: The student must identify specific errors.

54

Decision Making Task

Background Information:

Discrimination is the unfair treatment of certain people for reasons such as their religion, skin color, physical disabilities, or country of origin. In the late 1800's and early 1900's, Chinese immigrants were victims of discrimination in the United States. Laws were passed that purposefully discriminated against the Chinese. An example is given below.

The Pigtail Ordinance

In China, a man's queue was an important tradition. A queue is the long braid that hangs from the back of the head. During the 1870's, a law was passed called the Pigtail Ordinance. The law said that any Chinese man found guilty of a crime would have his queue cut off. This law applied only to Chinese people.

Your Task:

It is not easy to understand why lawmakers of the time found it necessary to pass the Pigtail Ordinance. You are asked to consider the factors that may have caused them to pass such a law. You are also asked to think about how the Pigtail Ordinance discriminates against the Chinese. Finally, you are asked to consider how this law may have affected Chinese immigration to the United States. Your answers should be recorded on the activity sheet provided.

Decision Making Task Activity Sheet

Name _____

Date _____

1. List the factors that you think may have caused lawmakers to pass the Pigtail Ordinance.

   _____

   _____

   _____

   _____

2. In what ways does the Pigtail Ordinance discriminate against Chinese?

   _____

   _____

   _____

   _____

3. What effects could the Pigtail Ordinance have had on Chinese immigration?

   _____

   _____

   _____

   _____

Decision Making Task Rubric

Score 3:

◇ The student clearly articulates the factors causing lawmakers to pass the Pigtail Ordinance.

◇ The student clearly articulates the ways the law discriminates against Chinese.

◇ The student clearly articulates the effects the law had on Chinese immigration.

Score 2:

◇ The student has a basic understanding of the factors causing lawmakers to pass the Pigtail Ordinance.

◇ The student has a basic understanding of how the law discriminates against Chinese.

◇ The student has a basic understanding of the effects the law had on Chinese immigration.

Score 1:

◇ The student did not understand the factors causing the law to be passed.

◇ The student did not understand how the law discriminates against Chinese.

◇ The student did not understand the effects the law had on Chinese immigration.

Score 0:

◇ The student did not respond to the task.

Problem Solving Task

Problem Solving Task

Background Information:

Lung disease, heart disease, cancer—these can be the results of smoking cigarettes, the U.S. surgeon general warned years ago. Recently we learned something more alarming. Not only do smokers harm themselves, but they also poison the air around them. The burning tobacco and the exhaled smoke contain pollutants which damage the health of nearby persons breathing the same air. Many such people are now suffering the same illnesses which afflict smokers themselves. Mighty efforts are being made to lower air pollution from cars and factories, but what can we do about second-hand smoke pollution from tobacco?

Wrapped in colorful plastic and aluminum, hundreds of inviting products line our supermarket shelves. The wrapping and containers are often more costly and attractive than their contents. Once purchased and discarded, however, these attractive containers often become eyesores. Take a look around your neighborhood, your school, the beach, and the countryside. Do we suffer from trash pollution? Such solid waste—especially plastic and aluminum—may last for years before decaying. What can we do about this type of pollution?

Your Task:

You have just read examples of two types of pollution. Your task is to create a poster to display in your school or neighborhood offering suggestions for controlling pollution. First, brainstorm some basic actions the average citizen can take to control pollution. Then design your poster to capture attention, inform citizens, and offer solutions. Use the activity sheet provided to help you organize for the task.

Problem Solving Task
Activity Sheet

Name_____ Date _____

1. What type of pollution will you focus on? _____
   _____

2. What are some possible solutions for controlling the pollution?_____
   _____
   _____

3. What basic information do you want to give citizens about pollution?_____
   _____
   _____

4. Sketch a poster design that will capture the attention of the citizens.

Problem Solving Task Rubric

Score 3:

◇ The student clearly defined the pollution problem.

◇ The student offered several practical, viable solutions to the pollution problem.

◇ The student created a poster that would focus attention to the pollution problem.

Score 2:

◇ The student basically defined the pollution problem.

◇ The student offered a practical solution to the pollution problem.

◇ The student created a poster that would focus attention to the pollution problem.

Score 1:

◇ The student did not clearly define the pollution problem.

◇ The student offered an impractical solution to the pollution problem.

◇ The student created a poster that would not necessarily focus attention to the pollution problem.

Score 0:

◇ The student did not respond to the task.

Invention Task

Background Information:

If you had been one of the founding fathers of our country, what would you have chosen as our national symbol? Benjamin Franklin thought a turkey should be our national symbol. Others, however thought the eagle was a better symbol of the freedom and power of our nation. Hence, the bald eagle became our national symbol. We have other national symbols, such as the Liberty Bell. The Liberty Bell is a symbol of liberty or freedom. The flag is a symbol showing we are one nation made up of separate states.

Your Task:

Imagine that you have been chosen to design a special symbol for a national holiday. First, research the origins of the national holiday. You can record your findings on the activity sheet provided. Then, design a memorable symbol that represents the holiday. You may draw your symbol on the same activity sheet. For this project you may choose any national holiday from the list below.

National Holidays

Martin Luther King, Jr. Day
Presidents' Day
Memorial Day
Independence Day
Labor Day
Columbus Day
Veterans' Day
Thanksgiving Day

Invention Task
Activity Sheet

Name _____ Date _____

1. Explain the origin of the national holiday you selected.

   _____

   _____

   _____

2. In the circle draw a symbol to represent the national holiday that people will remember.

Invention Task Rubric

Score 3:

◇ The student clearly understood and communicated the origin of the national holiday selected.

◇ The student created a symbol that clearly represents the spirit of the national holiday.

◇ The student created a memorable symbol for the holiday.

Score 2:

◇ The student adequately communicated the origin of the national holiday selected.

◇ The student created a symbol that adequately represents the national holiday.

◇ The student created a clever symbol for the holiday.

Score 1:

◇ The student was not able to communicate the origin of the national holiday selected.

◇ The student created a symbol that did not relate to the holiday.

◇ The student did not create a memorable symbol for the holiday.

Score 0:

◇ The student did not respond to the task.

Create a Task

Background Information:

Other Information:

Your Task:

Create a Rubric

Type of task _____

Score 3:

Score 2:

Score 1:

Score 0:

Performance Task
Recording Sheet

Name _____

NAME	Comparison Task	Classification Task	Position Support Task	Application Task	Analyzing Perspectives Task	Decision Making Task	Historical Perspective Task	Predictive Task	Problem Solving Task	Experimental Task	Invention Task	Error Analysis Task

Individual Student
Performance Task Recording Sheet

Student's Name _____

Date _____   Grade Level _____

Type of Performance Task _____

Description of Task:

Student's Strengths:

Student's Weaknesses:

Assist student with:

Getting Started _____

Rationale

Cooperative investigations in social studies require students to work in heterogeneous groups toward a common goal on a particular task. Cooperative investigations encourage students to become partners in learning rather than competitors. Working in heterogeneous groups allows students to learn both with and from each other.

In cooperative investigations each student has a particular job or responsibility to the group. Therefore each student must make a contribution to successfully complete the task. It is important that each develops skills necessary for working with others. Research shows that these skills are valuable now and later as students become working adults.

How to use Cooperative Investigations

Cooperative investigations must be structured so that all students have an important role in the completion of the task. It is also important that groups are heterogeneously organized, not organized according to ability. The best group size at the third and fourth grade level is about three to four students. Groups should be ability, gender, and racially balanced as much as possible.

Once you have determined the participants in each group, you can assign them their roles. Four basic roles are described below:

> **Reader:** Reads all directions and sees that they are followed. (This role is optional.)
>
> **Recorder:** Writes group answers.
>
> **Manager:** Divides up the group work, distributes materials, and keeps everyone on task.
>
> **Leader:** Leads discussions and keeps everyone involved.

Students within the groups, as well as the teacher, can evaluate the effectiveness of each group member in relation to the completion of the assigned task.

This section includes examples of three types of cooperative investigations. The first is a general group task and can be found on page 71. In this investigation students work cooperatively to create a state jeopardy type game.

Getting Started (cont.) _____

The second investigation included in this guide is a "jigsaw" activity. The example can be found on page 72. In a jigsaw each student becomes an expert on a particular topic that is related to a larger project. Then the student shares that knowledge with his or her "home" group. To organize a jigsaw activity, you first need to identify several topics that are related to a larger topic or concept. Then set up an "expert" group for each smaller topic made up of one member from each "home" team. The expert group works together to research their topic. "Experts" then return to their "home" teams to share the fruits of their research with the others. The "home" teams then complete a final project such as a paper or oral presentation. The jigsaw activity in this resource guide relates to Native American stories.

The third type of cooperative investigation included in this guide is simulations. Simulations get students actively involved in history by participating in problem-solving dilemmas relating to causes and implications of historical events. The simulation places the student in the middle of a situation relevant to a famous episode in history. An example of a simulation can be found on page 73. It requires students to participate as Pilgrims in a harvest festival.

Using the Forms in This Section

General Group Task: State Jeopardy Game, Page 71

This is an example of a general group task that requires all students in the group to actively participate in a common goal. This example asks students to create questions and answers for a state jeopardy game. State topics for students to research include: state history, famous people from our state, state geography, state resources, state leaders, state symbols, state potpourri.

Getting Started (cont.) _____

Jigsaw Cooperative Task: Native American Stories, Page 72

In this example students must become experts on a particular Native American story. Then the experts retell, with details, their Native American story to the home group. The final task is for the home group to make a mural depicting Native American life based on what they learned from the stories.

Simulation Task: Pilgrim Feast, Page 73

This simulation asks students to plan and take part in a Pilgrim harvest festival.

Group Process Evaluation, Page 74

This form allows each participant in the group to evaluate the group's overall performance on the cooperative investigation task. Students are also asked to describe the group's strengths and frustrations, and to identify one way in which the group could improve their effectiveness.

Cooperative Learning Peer Evaluation, Page 75

This form allows students to evaluate the performance of each member of their group on their particular task. Students are asked to rate each member of the group as effective or ineffective and to provide supporting comments as well. This form could also be used by the teacher.

Teacher Evaluation for Cooperative Groups, Page 76

As you observe the cooperative groups in action, you can assess their effectiveness by completing this evaluation form. You are asked to observe how decisions are made, if the students were helping each other, if it was necessary for you to intervene, and if the group met their task objective. There is additional room provided for you to comment on individual members of the group.

Cooperative Investigations

General Group Task: State Jeopardy Game

Name _____

Members of your group _____

State Jeopardy is a fun and challenging game. In cooperative groups you will create the questions and answers for one category of the State Jeopardy game. Then, you will have the opportunity to play the game as a class.

State Categories

State history
Famous people from the state
State geography
State resources
State leaders
State symbols
State potpourri

The Activity

Once you have been assigned your category, your group will conduct research on that topic. Based on that research you will create six questions designed to test the knowledge of your classmates on that topic. Write your questions and answers on index cards and turn them in to your teacher.

Jigsaw Cooperative Task: Native American Stories

Members of "home" group

_____

_____

_____

Members of "expert" group

_____

_____

_____

For this activity you will be reading stories from *The Stolen Appaloosa and Other Indian Stories* by Paul M. Levitt and Elissa S. Guralnick (Bookmakers Guild, 1988).

One person from each "home" group will be assigned to an "expert" group. Each "expert" group will read one story from *The Stolen Appaloosa*. A list of the stories from the book appears below.

After every person in the expert group has read the story, all members of the group will discuss it. Make sure that you clearly understand the story while discussing it in your expert group.

After you have discussed the story with your expert group, you may return to your home group. At this point you will tell your home group the story along with a detailed explanation of its meaning.

After everyone in your home group has told their story, you can begin working on your group mural. The mural should depict Native American life as it was described in the stories read by your group. Good luck!

Choose one of the stories from *The Stolen Appaloosa and Other Indian Stories*

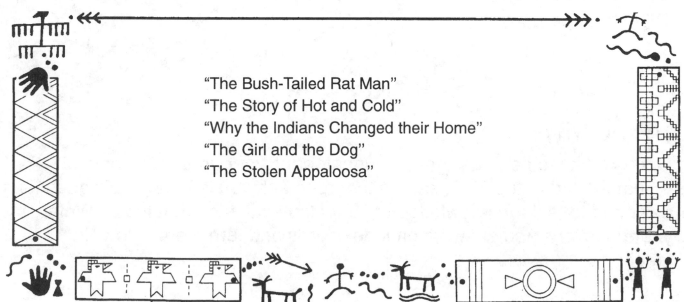

"The Bush-Tailed Rat Man"
"The Story of Hot and Cold"
"Why the Indians Changed their Home"
"The Girl and the Dog"
"The Stolen Appaloosa"

72

Simulation Task:
Pilgrim Feast

Winter was extremely harsh and difficult for the Pilgrims. Many died of pneumonia and tuberculosis. The Pilgrims looked forward to summer, the season of plenty. Corn ripened in the sun, and berries and pumpkins grew in abundance. To celebrate the plentiful harvest, the Pilgrims planned a harvest festival.

All of the Pilgrims contributed something to the feast. Some of the foods included deer meat, pumpkins, corn bread, corn pudding, berries, plums, wild turkeys, ducks, and geese. Today, this day of celebration is called Thanksgiving.

For this simulation you must imagine that you are a Pilgrim preparing for the first harvest feast. You should discuss as a class or in small groups the preparations for the special day as if you are all Pilgrims. What will you do or make for the festival? Foods made should be authentic for that time period. You should also choose a day for the festival.

When the special harvest day arrives, you should spend the day as a Pilgrim. Wear Pilgrim clothes and, if possible, use Pilgrim expressions when talking. Then have your feast and eat the foods you decided to make during your original planning meeting. You should also play games typical of that time period. Remember to try to stay in character as much as possible throughout the day!

Group Process Evaluation

Name _____

Date _____

Members of Your Group _____

_____

Cooperative Task _____

_____

1. Describe the effectiveness of your group on the task.

    _____

    _____

2. What were the group's strengths?

    _____

    _____

3. What frustrations did the group encounter?

    _____

    _____

4. Name one way in which your group could improve in order to be more effective on your next cooperative task.

    _____

    _____

Cooperative Learning Peer Evaluation

Name _____

Members of Your Group _____

Cooperative Task _____

Role	Effective	Ineffective	Comments
Reader			
Recorder			
Manager			
Leader			

Teacher Evaluation of Cooperative Groups

Cooperative task _____

Number of students in the group _____

Members of the group _____

_____

1. How were decisions made?

_____

_____

2. How did students help each other achieve a common goal?

_____

_____

3. Did you have to intervene at any time? If so, why?

_____

_____

4. Did the group meet the cooperative investigation objective? _____

Evidence or examples: _____

_____

Comments on individual group members:

_____

_____

_____

_____

_____

Getting Started _____

Rationale

Research projects give students the opportunity to study one topic for an extended period of time. Because students have the opportunity to focus on the single topic, they gain a much deeper understanding. In conducting the necessary research for their project, students practice important study and library skills such as getting the main idea, drawing conclusions, note taking, and the use of reference materials.

Not all research projects have to be long term. Students can do minimal research projects on current events. Most teachers have a time during the week in which students report on current events as part of the social studies curriculum. If students are given topics such as world events, community news, or sports, they can conduct a minimal bit of research using their daily newspaper. Now students learn basic research skills and become familiar with the organization of a newspaper.

One of the many benefits of research projects is the way in which oral communication skills can be integrated. Students can make oral presentations following a long term research project to report their findings to the class. Or, students can present their current event news to the class. Either way, students are practicing their public speaking skills which are clearly very important.

How to use Research Projects

Probably the most difficult skill for students to master in long term research projects is time management. The "Independent Research Contract" included in this section on page 79 can help students better manage their time for the project.

It will also be necessary to train students on oral presentation skills. Perhaps you could model appropriate public speaking skills by making a formal presentation to the class yourself. It may also be helpful if students were given a copy of the "Oral Presentation Evaluation" form on page 83. Students will then know what you are looking for when assessing their oral presentations.

Getting Started (cont.) _____

Using the Forms in This Section

Independent Research Contract, Page 79

This form can be used to help students better manage their time for the long term research project. Students are asked what they need to know and how they will go about obtaining that information. They are also asked to provide a time line to which you should strongly encourage them to adhere.

Research Project Cover Sheet, Page 80

This cover sheet is used to accompany the final draft of the student's research project. On it they are required to note their effectiveness in gathering information and communicating it in the report.

Research Project Evaluation: Individual Student, Page 81

You may use this form to evaluate a student's performance on the independent research project. You are asked to assess the student on five basic areas giving a score of 1 to 4. There is also room provided for examples or comments.

Research Project Evaluation: Class Record, Page 82

This form allows you to record the scores on all five basic areas assessed for each student in the class. Then, at a glance, you will know how all students did on the project. There is also room for you to make a brief comment for each student.

Oral Presentation Evaluation, Page 83

This evaluation form can be used when assessing the oral presentations students make to report their research findings to the class. Students are scored on a variety of public speaking skills. As mentioned earlier, you may wish to give a copy of this form to students so they will know in advance how their presentation will be scored.

Current Event Presentation Evaluation, Page 84

This form can be used to evaluate the oral presentation students give when reporting on their current event. Students are assessed on their ability to communicate the facts and significance of the event, to make the presentation interesting and informative, and to answer questions.

Independent Research Contract

Name _____

Date _____

The Project _____

My research topic is _____

_____

What do I need to know? _____

_____

Where will I get this information?_____

_____

_____

Time line: (Provide dates.)

I will begin my research _____

I will present a progress report _____

I will conclude my study _____

I will present my final report _____

Research Project Cover Sheet

Name _____

Date _____

Topic _____

Title of Research Project

_____

Describe how effective you were in gathering information for your project.

_____

_____

_____

Describe how effective you were in communicating your conclusions.

_____

_____

_____

Research Project Evaluation
Individual Student

Name _____

Research Project _____

(1 = poor 2 = average 3 = good 4 = excellent)

Skill	Score			
	1	2	3	4
Information obtained from several sources Examples:				
Project meets requirements Comments:				
Extras included (cover, pictures) Examples:				
Oral report given to class Comments:				
Extra credit work Examples:				

Research Project Evaluation:
Class Record

Project: _____

STUDENT NAME	Sources	Requirements	Extras	Oral Presentation	Extra Credit	COMMENTS

Oral Presentation Evaluation

Name _____

Date _____

Topic _____

Score: 1 = poor • 2 = average • 3 = good • 4 = excellent

1. The student speaks confidently. Score _____
   Comments: _____

   _____

2. The student expresses ideas with fluency. Score _____
   Comments: _____

   _____

3. The student answers questions. Score _____
   Comments: _____

   _____

4. The student maintains eye contact with the audience. Score _____
   Comments: _____

   _____

5. The student uses appropriate posture. Score _____
   Comments: _____

   _____

Areas for improvement: _____

_____

Additional Comments: _____

_____

Current Event Presentation Evaluation

Name _____

Date _____

Topic _____

Did the student convey the basic facts of the event accurately?

_____

_____

_____

Did the student convey the significance of the event?

_____

_____

_____

Was the presentation both interesting and informative?

_____

_____

_____

Was the student able to answer questions about the event?

_____

_____

_____

84

Getting Started _____

Rationale

Teachers in classrooms across the country are beginning to see learning as a joint venture between the teacher and the student. Naturally then, the responsibility for evaluation should also be shared between teacher and student. Self-evaluation makes the students aware of their own learning, progress, and growth throughout the school year. It is an indispensable part of any learning and assessment program that strives to have students take responsibility for their own learning.

Self-evaluation requires reflection, about not only academic work, but also attitude. Perhaps difficulty with social studies concepts has little to do with content, but rather much to do with motivation. By taking time to reflect, students can determine where their strengths and weaknesses lie and how to pinpoint what exactly is causing any difficulty.

How to Use Student Self-Evaluation

We cannot expect students to jump right into self-evaluation; they must be trained. Traditionally, students do the work and wait for the teacher to return it with a letter grade. Evaluating your own work is not easy, and taking the responsibility for doing so is certainly a challenge. The forms in this resource guide will help students to gradually become engaged in the self-evaluation process. They are asked to reflect on their academic achievement and their attitude, both important learning components.

It is important for you to stress confidentiality with student self-evaluations. Students may be reluctant to self-report and self-assess accurately if they fear their answers will be made public.

Getting Started *(cont.)*

Using the Forms in This Section

Social Studies Concepts Self-Evaluation, Page 87

This form is very useful because it is so flexible. It can be used along with any topic you may be studying in social studies. Prior to reading the textbook, students are asked to identify what they already know about the topic they will be studying. They are asked to report on what they learned following their reading of the text. Then, they must evaluate what else they need to know about the topic prior to taking a test. This last question can be particularly helpful for test preparation.

Research Project Self-Evaluation, Page 88

This form works very nicely with the other assessment forms in the "Research Project" section of this resource guide. However, because this form is a self-evaluation, it has been included in this section. Students are asked to rate their performance in five different areas related to their long term research project. It may be interesting for you to compare the student's response to your own response on the similar form for teachers located in the "Research Project" section on page 81.

Assignment Self-Evaluation, Page 89

This form asks students to evaluate a specific assignment. Students are asked how they feel about the assignment, what they did best, and where they need to improve. They are also asked to give themselves a grade for the assignment. Notes students make regarding what needs improvement can be used for future self-evaluations and reflections.

Writing Evaluation for a Publication Piece, Page 90

Now that students are reading so much historical fiction, they should be encouraged to write a historical fiction piece of their own. These stories can then be published for the rest of the class to enjoy. When determining which story to publish, students can use this writing self-evaluation. This form requires students to justify their selection of a piece of writing for publication. Students are asked why the piece was chosen, what is the strongest part, what was most difficult about writing the story, and what makes it ready for publication.

Social Studies Concepts
Self-Evaluation

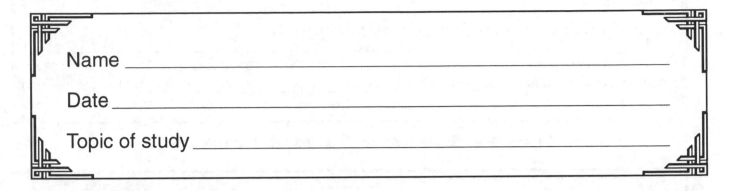

Name _____

Date _____

Topic of study _____

What do you already know about the topic?
(Complete this section prior to reading the textbook)

What did you learn about the topic?
(Complete this section after reading the text)

What else do you need to know about the topic?
(Complete prior to taking an exam on the topic)

Research Project Self-Evaluation

Name _____

Date _____

Topic of study _____

(1 = poor 2 = average 3 = good 4 = excellent)

Skill	Score			
	1	2	3	4
Chose topic Comments:				
Consulted reference books Examples:				
Wrote report to meet requirements Examples:				
Included extras (cover, pictures) Examples:				
Gave oral report Examples:				

Assignment Self-Evaluation

Name _____

Type of Assignment _____

Title of Assignment _____

1. How do you feel about this assignment?

   _____

   _____

   _____

2. What did you do best on this assignment?

   _____

   _____

   _____

3. What could you improve on this assignment?

   _____

   _____

   _____

4. What grade do you feel you deserve on this assignment and why?

   _____

   _____

   _____

Writing Evaluation for a Publication Piece

Name _____

Title of story _____

Historical time period _____

Why did you choose this story for publication?

_____

_____

What is the strongest part of the story?

_____

_____

What makes that part so strong?

_____

_____

What was the hardest part about writing this story?

_____

_____

Why is your story ready for publication?

_____

_____

_____

90

Getting Started _____

Rationale

We take great pains to keep the parents of our students informed regarding progress and classroom activities. Parents can be invited to take part in the evaluation of the child's growth and progress. The assessment cycle is then complete because all three participants in the student's education — teacher, student, and parent — have been involved in evaluation. Asking parents to take a more active role in evaluation will naturally lead them to become more involved in the student's homework. Home reading logs can help parents realize when their child is spending too much time playing or watching T.V. rather than reading their social studies text or a piece of historical fiction. Another benefit of parent evaluation is clearly seen at parent conference time. Parents are better informed and better able to discuss their child's progress. Now the conference is a two way conversation between teacher and parent, rather than a one way monologue performed by the teacher and directed at the parent.

How to use Parent Evaluations

Parents, like students, need to be adequately trained in how to evaluate. It may be worth your time to schedule a training session so parents can be informed about the process. Although it will take time to plan such a training session, in the long run you will get more and better information on the parent response forms if they are properly trained.

Using the Forms in This Section

Parent Questionnaire, Page 92

It is important for parents to consider their child's strengths and weaknesses in the classroom. They should also consider what goals they have for their child. This form will help parents plan the present and future of their child's education.

Home Reading Log, Page 93

Students can use this form to keep track of the textbook chapters and books they read at home as well as the time they spend reading. Parents are asked to verify the entries made by students.

Parent Questionnaire

Student's Name

Age _____ Grade _____ Date _____

Name of parent completing form:

Please answer the questions as they relate to the study of history/social studies.

1. What is going well for your child this year? _____
   _____

2. What progress has your child made since the beginning of the school year?
   _____
   _____

3. Do you have any concerns about your child?
   _____
   _____

4. Do you have any suggestions for working with your child?
   _____
   _____

5. What are your goals for your child this school year?
   _____
   _____

Additional Comments: _____
_____
_____

Thank you for your time!

Parent Evaluation

Home Reading Log

Student's Name _____

Name of parent verifying form: _____

Please verify the time your child spends reading the social studies text or books related to social studies at home.

Date	Title of Book/Chapter	Pages	Time Start	Time Stop	Parent Sign

Thanks for your time!

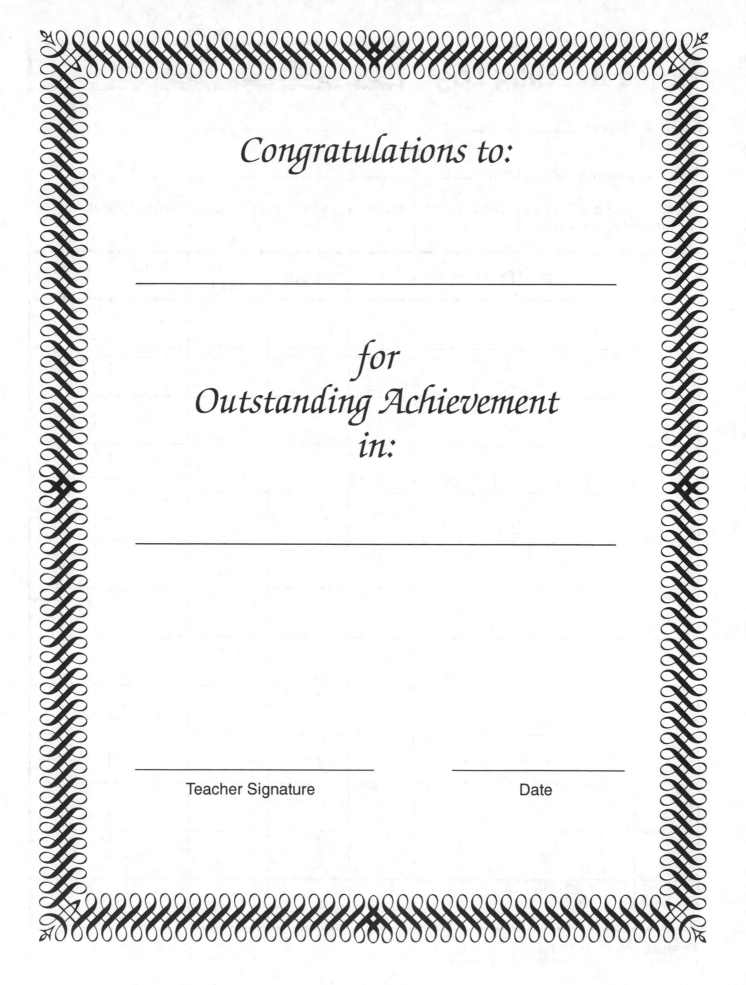

Congratulations to:

_____

for
Outstanding Achievement
in:

_____

_____   _____
Teacher Signature   Date

Generic Record Sheet

Social Studies Assessment Bibliography

Braun, Joseph A. "Social Technology in the Elementary Social Studies Curriculum." *Social Education.* November/December, 1992: 389-392.

Evans, Michael D. "Manifest Destiny: Understanding Through Simulation." *Social Education.* February, 1993: 89-90.

Finkelstein, Judith M., Lynn E. Nielsen, and Switzer, Thomas. "Primary Elementary Social Studies Instruction: A Status Report." *Social Education.* February, 1993: 64-69.

Goodman, Kenneth S., Lois Bird Bridges, and Yetta M. Goodman. *The Whole Language Catalog Supplement on Authentic Assessment.* Macmillan, 1992

Gustafson, Kraig. "Government in Action: A Simulation." *Social Education.* February, 1993: 90-92.

Herman, Joan L., Pamela R. Aschbacher, and Lynn Winters. *A Practical Guide to Alternative Assessment.* Association for Supervision and Curriculum Development, 1992.

Hill, Bonnie Campbell. *Practical Aspects of Authentic Assessment: Putting the Pieces Together.* Christopher-Gordon Publishers, 1994.

Jasmine, Julia. *Portfolio Assessment for Your Whole Language Classroom.* Teacher Created Materials. 1992.

Jasmine, Julia. *Portfolios and Other Assessments.* Teacher Created Materials, 1993.

Marzano, Robert J., Debra Pickering, and Jay McTighe. *Assessing Student Outcomes.* Association for Supervision and Curriculum Development, 1993

Perrone, Vito. *Expanding Student Assessment.* Association for Supervision and Curriculum Development, 1993.

Routman, Regie. *Invitations.* Heinemann, 1991

Routman, Regie. *Transitions.* Heinemann, 1988.

Tierney, Robert J., Mark A.Carter, and Laura E. Desai. *Portfolio Assessment in the Reading-Writing Classroom.* Christopher Gordon Publishers, 1991.

Tunnell, Michael O., and Richard Ammon (Eds.). *The Story of Ourselves: Teaching History Through Children's Literature.* Heinemann, 1993